JORDAN

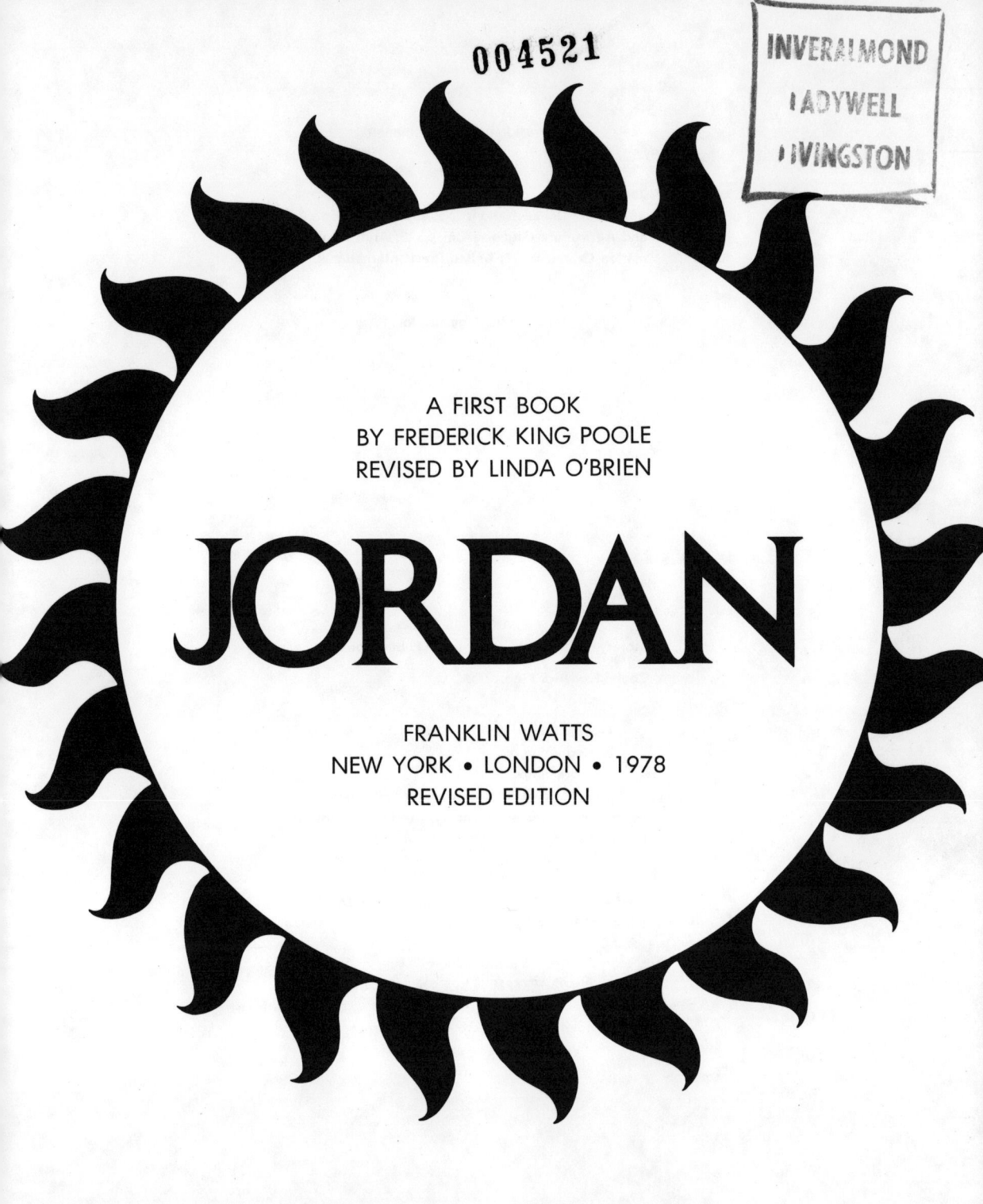

A FIRST BOOK
BY FREDERICK KING POOLE
REVISED BY LINDA O'BRIEN

JORDAN

FRANKLIN WATTS
NEW YORK • LONDON • 1978
REVISED EDITION

Cover design by Jackie Schuman

Photographs courtesy of:
Jordan Ministry of Information: pp. 9, 11, 34,
48, 51, 54; United Nations: pp. 18, 21; UN/Food
and Agriculture Organization: p. 23; Arab Information Center: p. 27; United Press International:
p. 41.

Maps by Vantage Art, Inc.

Library of Congress Cataloging in Publication Data

Poole, Frederick King.
    Jordan.

    (A First book)
    Bibliography: p.
    Includes index.
    SUMMARY: A discussion of Jordan's history,
people, government, economy, land, and posi-
tion in the ongoing Arab-Israeli conflict.
    1. Jordan—Juvenile literature. [1. Jordan]
I. O'Brien, Linda. II. Title.
DS153.P66   1978   956.95'04   78-16652
ISBN 0-531-02241-2

6   5   4   3   2

CONTENTS

JORDAN

AN INDEPENDENT PEOPLE

There is a land, at the eastern end of the Mediterranean, at the northernmost tip of the Red Sea, covering the western edge of the great Arabian Desert. Through it the Jordan River runs down to the Dead Sea and to the great valley of Wadi Araba. It is a place of valleys and mountains, wilderness and field, soft green oasis and harsh, stony desert. The land is Jordan.

For 4,000 years Jordan has been a crossroads journeyed by other civilizations. It lies close to the area that was the Fertile Crescent, the land between the Tigris and Euphrates rivers, which was probably the first land that people ever cultivated. There, people learned how to work the land in a systematic way, tilling the fields and growing the crops they needed. On the western side of the Jordan the land goes down to the sea, where fishermen brought in all the wonderful fish of the Mediterranean. The fishermen became sailors, venturing farther and farther from

(1)

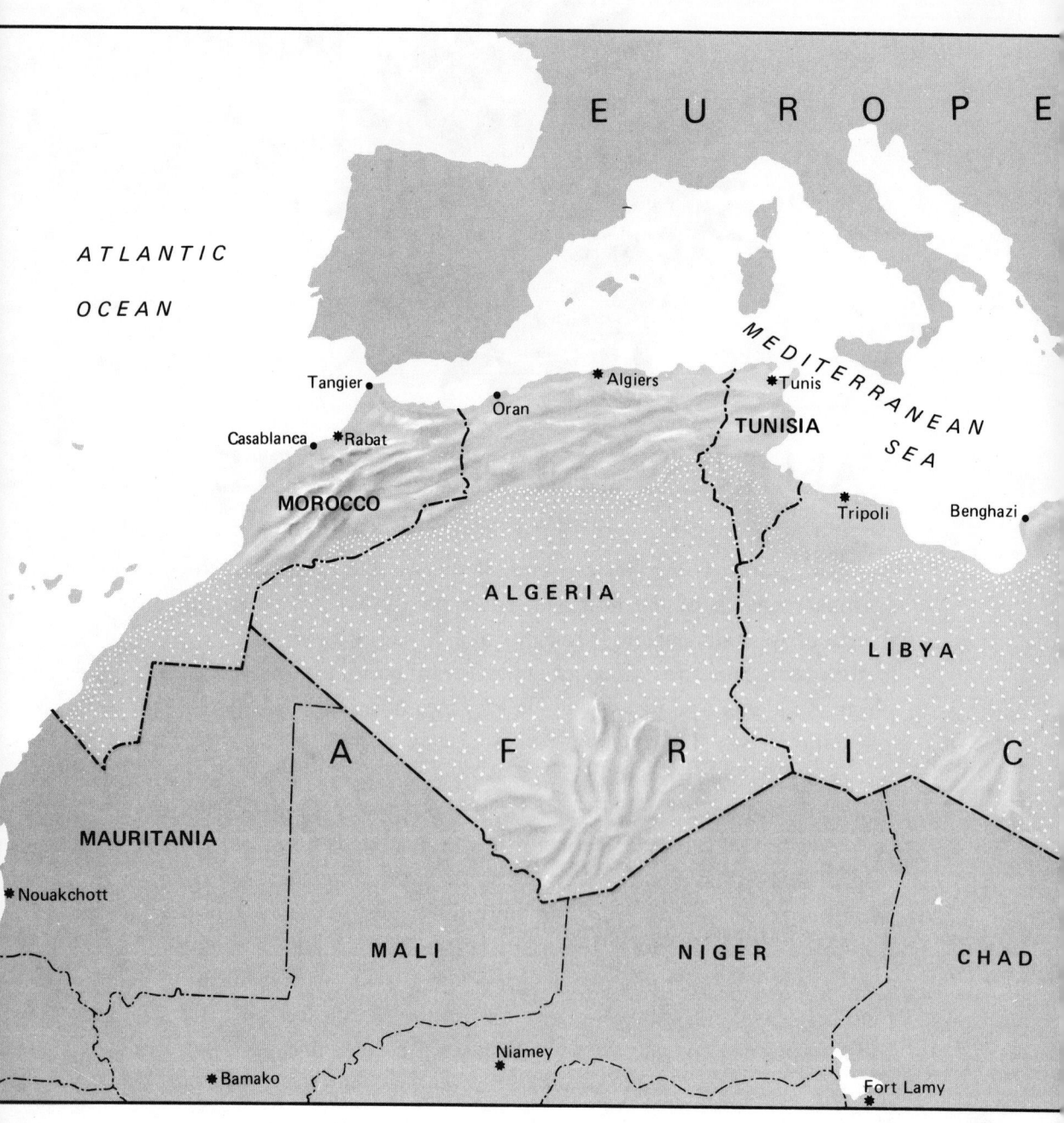

their own shores to explore and visit the other coasts of the Mediterranean. The farmers became craftsmen, blacksmiths, and weavers, with merchandise as well as food to sell. The merchants voyaged farther from home, east to Persia, south to Egypt, and west to the Mediterranean ports. The land around the Jordan River, with water in rivers and oases, became a popular route for traders. The people who lived along the river became used to strangers from different lands, who had different customs and spoke different languages. They became "sophisticated," used to ways different from their own, as people from all countries and cultures passed along the trade route.

In the desert lived the tribes who were wise in its ways, the Bedouin people. They learned to follow the path of the seasons, grazing their herds of camels, goats, or sheep on the few green plants found in the desert in the winter. In the hot, dry summer they moved to mountains, oases, or river valleys to find the plants there, and in the next summer they moved back to the desert again. There was never much grass to find, so the tribes moved on as the herds ate all that there was. The Bedouin learned how to live in the desert, to survive in its harsh climate. Few other people dared even go into the desert, much less try to live there, so the Bedouin developed a strong sense of independence and pride in their ability to take care of themselves. They became fierce warriors, ready to defend their territory and their families against any threat. They rode camels and horses superbly, were loyal to their families above all else, and fought ferociously when they thought it was necessary.

And this land and these people still exist today. They live modern lives in our modern world, but they still have much in common with their ancestors. These people are the Arabs — Bedouin and Palestinians. The land is Jordan.

THE LAND: VALLEY AND DESERT

In almost any country, one of the most important things is the land. The land determines what crops people can grow, what minerals or other natural resources they can use, and whether it is hard or easy to live there. In Jordan, it is often hard.

Jordan covers an area of about 38,000 square miles (98,500 sq km). This includes the slightly more than 2,000 square miles (5,200 sq km) of the West Bank, the area on the western side of the Jordan River now occupied by Israel.

Jordan's entire western frontier is with Israel. The other frontiers are along the desert portions of other Arab nations, and often they are hardly marked at all. To the north is Syria and to the northeast, Iraq. To the east and south is Saudi Arabia, the largest Arab country. To the southwest, past Israel, is Egypt, the most populous Arab nation. Often, relations between all these countries and Jordan have been unfriendly or strained.

(5)

Tripoli •

Baalbek •

Beirut ★
LEBANON
Sidon •
R.

Tyre •

Acre •

Haifa •
Nazareth •

Sea of Galilee

Golan Heights

S Y R I A

★ Damascus

Litani

MEDITERRANEAN SEA

West Bank
• Irbid

Tel Aviv - Jaffa •
Nablus •

J O R D A N

Jerusalem ★
• Amman
Zarqa •
★

Gaza •
Gaza Strip
△
Hebron •

• Port Said
Masada ∴
Dead Sea

Beersheba •
Karak •
ISRAEL

Jordan

I R A Q

**S A U D I
A R A B I A**

Suez Canal

E G Y P T

• Suez
△
△

SINAI PENINSULA
(Occupied by Israel)

Ma'an •

Gulf of Suez

△

△

△

Elath •
• Aqaba

Gulf of Aqaba

△

• Sharm el Sheikh

△	Oil field
— · —	Oil pipeline
∴	Ancient ruins

Israel lies between Jordan and the Mediterranean, but Jordan does have access to a sea at Aqaba. This port, in the far southwest region of the country, is at the head of the Gulf of Aqaba, an inlet of the Red Sea which leads to the Indian Ocean.

You can picture how the land of Jordan looks. Think of the land as a flat tabletop, tilted up at one side. The side that is tilted up is the western edge of the country. Over the steep edge of the tabletop is the great Rift Valley, containing the Jordan River, the Dead Sea, and the Wadi Araba. The high, tilted edge of the tabletop includes the highlands and mountains that run north and south along the edge of the Rift. And the flat section, sloping gradually down, is the flat steppe land and desert that goes from the highlands, south and east to the desert, running flat across the whole Arabian peninsula to the Arabian Sea.

THE RIFT VALLEY

The two most important features in Jordan's geography are the desert to the east, and the Rift Valley in the west. This great valley, also known as the Great Rift or the Jordanian Rift, is a deep depression running north to south along the entire length of the country. There are stretches of highlands along either side of the Rift. Those on the east are controlled by Jordan and those on the west by Israel.

The Rift Valley begins in the north at the fertile Jordan River valley, which is 65 miles (104 km) long. The name Jordan is from the Hebrew word *yordan*, like the Arabic word *urdunn*, which means "the descender." And the river does descend, from its source in Syria 1,000 feet (305 m) above sea level, to where it ends in the Dead Sea, whose surface is 1,292 feet (394 m) below

(7)

sea level. For two-thirds of its length, in fact, the river is below sea level. The flood plain of the Jordan River and the Dead Sea is called the Ghor. Where it is irrigated, the soil is well-suited to growing a variety of vegetables and fruits.

The Dead Sea continues south from the Jordan River. It lies in the deepest depression of land on the surface of the earth, and it is 1,000 feet (305 m) deep in some places. The sea is "dead" because evaporation into the hot air leaves its waters so full of minerals that no animal or plant life can live there.

South of the Dead Sea is the Wadi Araba. *Wadi* means a small valley or gully that is dry except when it rains. From the Dead Sea, the Wadi Araba rises to a high point about 75 feet (23 m) above sea level, and then it drops southward to the Gulf of Aqaba. The farther south it goes, the more barren the countryside is.

TOWARD THE DESERT

All the land that can be cultivated and used to grow crops of food is located in a narrow strip of land running north to south, just east of the Rift Valley highlands. Past this narrow strip the land flows into the desert, becoming drier, browner, and less inhabited, until it stretches into the Syrian desert in the north and the Arabian desert in the south.

*The Jordan River, located
in the Rift Valley, provides
water for the irrigation
of nearby farmland.*

Farthest north along this strip is the Yarmus River, which forms part of the border with Syria. It is the major tributary of the Jordan River. South of it is the Zarqa River, which also flows into the Jordan. Its name means blue, and it is a light blue shade where it runs over a stony bed. Both rivers are used in projects with dams, water storage, irrigation canals, and hydroelectric power. Between them is a district called Ajlun, around Irbid, a rapidly growing agricultural and commercial city. This area has craggy mountains with rushing streams, limestone and sandstone outcropping, and fertile valleys. It contains most of the country's pine forests and some areas of scrub oak trees. Eastward are fields of wheat and barley, beans and corn. Past these fields is the beginning of the desert.

Between the Zarqa River and the Wadi Mojib, the forest areas end and the mountains widen out to an open tableland. This region contains the districts of Balqa and Amman. Amman, the capital city, has gone through great periods of history, and still has a well-preserved arena from the days of the Romans. In 1921 Amman was just a small town, with 6,000 inhabitants. Today it is a bustling modern city, with over 600,000 people. Zarqa, just north of Amman, was also a village; it now has a population of over 250,000 people.

Between the Wadi Mojib and the Wadi Hasa is the ancient district of Moab, now called Karak. This is a nearly unbroken plateau which slopes gradually down to the desert to the east. This is the southernmost area that is important for cultivation. In ancient times it was noted for its wine and fruit, and it exported cattle, camels, goats, and sheep. Karak wheat is still highly regarded. In the fortified town of Karak, a twelfth-century castle built by the Crusaders still stands.

The desert of Ma'an, considered to be one of the most spectacular deserts in the world.

South of the Karak district is the district of Ma'an, which stretches down to the Gulf of Aqaba. It is a wild and sparsely populated area. Once it was covered with forest, but the trees were all cut down long ago to make fires for cooking and heating, and to provide railway ties and steam engine fuel for the old Hejaz Railway. The desert of Ma'an may be the most spectacular desert anywhere. It includes the Wadi Rumm, a valley studded with multishaded sandstone mesas, where T. E. Lawrence and the Arab fighters camped during World War I, and the Jebel Rumm (*jebel* means hill or mountain), Jordan's highest peak, which rises to 5,755 feet (1,755 m) above sea level. It also contains the city of Petra, a beautiful, ancient city carved out of the rose-hued rock cliffs by the Nabateans, an Arab people who lived there in Roman times.

THE WEST BANK

The land between the Jordan River and the Mediterranean Sea, where the country of Israel now lies, has been called Palestine since the days of the Romans.

West of the Jordan River and the northern half of the Dead Sea is the small but heavily populated area called the West Bank. This area was part of Jordan, but it was captured by the Israelis in the 1967 war, and it is still occupied by them. The West Bank is a highland region, whose only river is the Jordan. It had been a poor section of the country, but more and more land was being cultivated and industries were being developed. The West Bank contains the old part of the city of Jerusalem, including the major holy places of the Jewish, Muslim, and Christian religions. It also contains the Holy Land towns and the cities of Bethlehem (where

Christ was born), Nablus, Hebron, and Jericho, the oldest inhabited walled city in the world.

WEATHER, PLANTS, AND ANIMALS

In the populated western areas of Jordan, the long summers are generally pleasant. The temperature rarely rises above 85° F (29° C) in the daytime. At night, it is usually about 65° F (18° C). In the winter, temperatures rarely drop below freezing, but sometimes there is snow in Amman. The Jordan River valley's climate is like that of the Mediterranean, and it is hotter in the summer and milder in the winter. Sometimes in the spring a hot, dry wind, called the *khamsin*, blows across the valley from the eastern desert, carrying fine desert dust and making the temperature rise above 120° F (49° C). The desert areas are very hot. During the day the temperature — in the shade — is more than 100° F (38° C). It cools off considerably at night, and the desert winters can be quite cold.

There is very little rainfall anywhere in Jordan. Summers are dry all over the country. Most years, the winter rainy season starts in November and lasts through March or April. In the Jordan River valley there may be as much as 40 inches (102 cm) of rain a year, and more than 16 inches (41 cm) in the more fertile areas of the highlands. But east of the mountains the rainfall drops off gradually to about 4 inches (10 cm), and in the desert it is sometimes less than 1 inch (2.56 cm).

The vegetation in Jordan varies according to the rainfall. The wetter highlands have pine and oak trees, but the dry wadis have only scrub growth. The plateaus and slopes are green only during

(13)

the rainy season. In the spring, flowers bloom throughout the highlands and even in parts of the desert. Desert oases have many different kinds of palm trees, the only kind of tree that can live there.

Crops are raised in the strip of cultivated land just east of the Jordan River valley. In the Ghor, olives and citrus fruits are grown, and vegetables are also raised in the valleys. Elsewhere, the main crops are cereals, particularly wheat, barley, and corn. And anywhere that there is any kind of vegetation, there are herds of sheep and goats.

There is still a lot of wildlife in Jordan. The ibex, a mountain goat with long, curving horns, is occasionally seen south of the Dead Sea. There are some hyenas, wildcats, and panthers in the rugged highlands and some gazelles in the desert. The desert is also home to many small animals, such as the mole rat. Poisonous scorpions are common, as are mosquitoes. Swarms of locusts sometimes damage the crops. There are many wild birds, including partridges, pigeons, and ducks, as well as some vultures and eagles.

RESOURCES

Unlike other Arab countries, Jordan does not have a wealth of natural resources. So far, explorations for oil have been unsuccessful. Phosphates, used for fertilizers, are dug from the earth at Ruseifa, northeast of Amman, and at Hasa, in the south. They are Jordan's single most important export. Large deposits of potash, also valuable for fertilizer, have been discovered in the Dead Sea but have not yet been used. There are also a few copper deposits.

What industries exist are mostly for the Jordanians themselves. These include food processing and the manufacture of soap, batteries, shoes, cigarettes, and paper. There is a large cement factory, and a few fertilizer, glass, and ceramic factories. But Jordan has always imported more items, both food and manufactured goods, than it has exported.

Throughout its history as a modern state, Jordan has relied heavily on foreign aid to help it pay for all its imports. This aid is now mostly from the United States, with Great Britain and various European countries also participating. The government hopes that its plans for developing industries can make the economy of Jordan as self-sufficient as its people have always been.

THE PEOPLE

Most Jordanians are modern people in the way they live, but their Bedouin tradition remains an important factor in their lives. Most east Jordanians and many of those born in west Jordan are descendants of the Bedouin. Bedouin means "inhabitant of the desert," and it was in the desert that the Bedouin way of life developed.

In 1921, at least half the people of Jordan were living in Bedouin goat hair tents. Some of these nomads spent part of the year cultivating patches of land, but most were on the move almost constantly, taking their goats and sheep in search of water and grass. Their main source of income was breeding camels and horses.

Today, only a small number of Jordan's people are nomads. Most now live in stone houses in villages, towns, or cities. Their social structure, though, still comes from desert tribal arrangements, and their customs are related to the ancient ideas of family obligations and rules of hospitality.

THE BEDOUIN

Life in the desert is harsh. Surviving is difficult in a land where the nearest water may be miles and miles away. A person alone is completely helpless. For the Bedouin, the family is most important, for it is with the family's protection and help that each person lives and prospers.

The Bedouin family is patriarchal: that is, the father is the ruler of the family. Bedouin think of a "family" as a man, his wife, his sons, their wives and children, and his unmarried daughters. When a woman marries, she becomes part of her husband's family. The father makes all the decisions for the family, and he is respected and obeyed by everyone in it. A family lives together, in the same tent or house, or right next to each other. As a man becomes too old to act as head of the family, the son who has displayed the most ability gradually becomes the new family head. The other sons may leave to head their own families, but they will probably still stay very close by, in the same nomad group or the same village.

THE ALL-IMPORTANT FAMILY

Family relationships are very important. Bedouin are proud to trace their families' lineages back to strong and famous leaders. A tribe is based on families that are descended from common ancestors. The *sheik*, or "head," of the tribe, is thought of as being the

father of the tribe, and he has the same strong authority over a tribe as a father has over his family. However, each sheik usually has a council of men from the tribe that advises him, and he would find it very difficult to act against its wishes.

This same pattern of patriarchal authority is seen in all parts of Jordanian society. Many Jordanians, for instance, feel great loyalty to their king because he is the most powerful of the sheiks, ruling over all the tribes, the respected "father" of the country.

With men considered so important, women have never had a strong role in Bedouin society. A woman was regarded as the mother of her son or the wife of her husband, but she was not credited for anything she herself did. Women were kept within the household, in the tent or in the house. They were in charge of the home and, of course, they could exert some influence over their husbands and children. This is one aspect of Bedouin life that is changing. Now, women are becoming more independent, getting an education, and working in jobs outside the home. But they are still closely sheltered by their fathers or brothers and bow to their families' decisions.

BEDOUIN HOSPITALITY

Another important part of surviving in the desert was helping and protecting others in it. Just as early American pioneers, aware of

Though most Jordanians now live a settled life in towns and villages, some maintain a nomadic lifestyle, leading their livestock from water hole to water hole.

the dangers of a hostile land, welcomed any stranger to their homes, so the Bedouin believe that they must shelter any who come to them. People roaming the desert can go up to any tent and ask for hospitality. The owner of the tent is automatically under the obligation of sheltering and feeding them for three successive days and nights. The host is also under an obligation to protect his guest. It is unforgivable, for example, for any other guest to insult him. This hospitality is a matter of duty, and no Bedouin takes it lightly.

A VANISHING WAY OF LIFE

There are fewer and fewer nomad tribes today. There has always been a pattern of people moving from the desert to settled communities, because the desert cannot support many people. Recently, the introduction of cars and trucks has cost the Bedouin their traditional livelihood as horse and camel breeders. Today horses are needed only by sportsmen or for ceremonial use by the army. Some camels are still used to transport goods, and they are also a source of food for the poor, but the Bedouin can no longer live by trading them. The government has also given these people land to farm to help increase the supply of food.

Perhaps most important, the government has made a great effort to attract the Bedouin to service in the military forces. Nomads often raided villages or fought wars between tribes. The government thought that the best way to end this, but to still keep the Bedouin's great pride in their ability as warriors, was to put these skills into the service of the country. Today Jordan's Arab Army is dominated by Bedouins, many of them from tribes noted for their loyalty to the king. The army is probably the country's

A typical Bedouin goat-hair tent

greatest source of political stability, since any potential enemies of the king know that they would have to face these fierce and faithful soldiers.

THE PALESTINIANS

Palestinians, the people from the area between the Jordan River valley and the Mediterranean Sea, have always been a worldly and settled people, living in small villages or towns. But, every bit as much as Bedouin, they think of themselves as Arabs.

Palestinians left their homes in great numbers during and after the Arab-Israeli war that ended in 1949. Some who moved from Israel to Jordan's West Bank, and to the Gaza Strip in the southwest corner of Israel, were displaced again in 1967 when the Israelis occupied these two areas. Some possessed skills that enabled them to make successful new lives abroad. Often, their level of education was higher than that of the people in countries where they moved. But many Palestinians became displaced, and frequently unwanted, refugees. A great many Palestinians live for the dream of one day returning to their homes, and consider themselves still at war with Israel.

There are about 3½ million Palestinians who have left their land. Some 1,150,000 live in east Jordan, the largest group anywhere. About 700,000 live in the West Bank, now occupied by Israel. This means that over half of Jordan's population consists of Palestinians, and this has often led to problems. There have been conflicts between the east Jordanians and the Palestinians, especially over continuing the fight to regain Palestine.

Some Palestinians organized themselves into groups to try to fight for their return to a land they consider theirs. The largest such

After the 1967 Israeli occupation of the West Bank,
thousands of Arabs fled to Palestinian
refugee camps in Jordan. Many live there still.

group is the Palestine Liberation Organization, or P.L.O. Some of the Palestinian groups engage in terrorist activities, such as bombing buildings and taking hostages, to publicize their beliefs and pressure the Arab and Israeli governments to meet their demands. In 1970, there was a vicious and complex civil war in Jordan in which the king was nearly overthrown. Most east Jordanians supported the king while some Palestinians sought his downfall. The king won, with the aid of loyal and well-trained Bedouin army troops. The P.L.O. and other Palestinian groups were banned from any activities in Jordan.

But the great majority of Palestinians, as much as they may long to return to their homes, are peaceful people, living through very hard times as best they can.

THE MINORITIES

Although Jordan is mainly an Islamic state, about 7 percent of its people are Christians. Their religious rights are protected by law, and they celebrate Christian holidays, especially Christmas and Easter, much as they would in a Christian nation. Most follow either the Armenian, Greek Orthodox, or Roman Catholic churches, but there are also a few Protestants.

The Armenians are the only Christian community of any size that does not consider itself to be Arab. Most of the Armenians are descended from those who came to the area in the late nineteenth and early twentieth centuries, or during World War I. Although few in number, they are highly visible since they are traditionally skilled artisans. Because Jordan does not have a long urban tradition, many of the people with urban skills — such as tailors, photographers, and shoemakers — are Armenians.

The people known as the Circassians form another small but important minority. They are Muslims whose homeland was once the Caucasus in Russia. These blond-haired, blue-eyed people came to Jordan in the nineteenth century and settled in towns in the north. They learned Arabic, but most also speak their own language, and they have their own social and cultural organizations. They, like the Bedouin, often hold key positions in the armed services, especially in the air force. The king has a personal Circassian guard, a vivid unit dressed in the old military uniform of the Caucasus, with black fur hats, long coats, riding boots, and long silver daggers.

CLOTHES

Jordanians are moving away from their traditional clothing. Most now go about in Western clothes. But even in the cities some people wear the garments that have been used since biblical times.

In the desert nearly every man wears the *kaffiyeh*, a shawl used as a headdress, held in place with a braided coil called an *agal*. In the winter, the kaffiyeh is usually of red and white or black and white heavy cloth and is good protection against the cold. The kaffiyeh that is worn in the summer is made of a white, gauzy fabric. Some kaffiyehs worn by royalty are embroidered with gold. The kaffiyeh is an extremely practical garment, especially for the desert. It can be wrapped around the face to filter out sand. It offers protection from mosquitoes as well as from the scorching desert sun. You can still see some people in kaffiyehs on the sidewalks of Amman.

Another practical Arab garment for the desert climate is the *abaya*, a long cloak with an open front and two holes at the sides for the arms. It is worn over a *thawb*, a long-sleeved, white shirt that goes down to the ankles. The abayas worn by Bedouin sheiks are black and embroidered with gold. Like the kaffiyeh, the abaya is no longer very common in the towns and cities, but it is still worn by village people and the Bedouin.

The women's equivalent of the abaya is a long-sleeved, ankle-length gown called the *kaftan*. Many have extremely elaborate embroidery work. Elegant Jordanian city women often wear kaftans as formal evening dress.

At one time most Jordanian women, like women in many other Muslim countries, wore veils for reasons of religion and modesty. Today in Jordan the veil is nearly extinct.

FOOD

The food that most people in Jordan eat is limited by the lack of fields and cropland. The meat most often eaten is lamb. There are some fresh vegetables, such as tomatoes and olives, and some potatoes, rice, and Arabic bread to round out the meals. But, especially in the country, away from large towns and city market-places, the diet is very simple.

One example of Bedouin culture that is still widespread in Jordan is the traditional Bedouin feast, known as a *mensef*. It is

The traditional Arab abaya, or cloak, and kaffiyeh. When wrapped around the face, the kaffiyeh protects the wearer from sun, sand, and insects.

served everywhere, at weddings, during religious festivals, or simply when someone wants to entertain a guest. It even forms the basis for official state banquets.

For the traditional mensef, an entire sheep is slaughtered. Its skin is saved to make the *farwa*, the long sheepskin coat worn by herdsmen. The sheep is cooked in a gigantic cauldron. Meanwhile, *jameed*, a sauce made from grated dried yogurt (called *leben*), is prepared. Flat bread is laid out on a large tray which is covered with rice. Parts of the sheep are placed around the rice, with the head in the middle. The jameed is poured over it, and the sheep is sprinkled with chopped parsley and fried nuts. Guests eat the mixture with their right hands. A servant is always around with a pitcher of water and soap for washing before and after the meal.

Occasionally the mensef is made with a goat or a camel, and outside the desert it is often made with chickens.

One custom of Bedouin hospitality is that of serving coffee. Whatever else visitors to Jordan are doing, they find themselves drinking coffee a large part of the time. The coffee beans are finely ground by hand with a mortar and pestle just before the coffee is made. Then the coffee, along with tasty ground cardamon seeds, is set in a curved brass pot over a charcoal fire for a long period of time. This strong brew is then served in tiny amounts, in small, handleless cups which are passed around and used by everyone. Coffee is served at all times of the day; before meals it is used as an appetizer and after meals as an aid to digestion.

A visitor must be careful to observe the rules. It is considered extremely impolite not to accept at least one cup of coffee, but it is greedy to drink more than three in a row. Until you signal that you are through by jiggling the empty cup back and forth, your cup will be refilled constantly, with true Bedouin hospitality.

ART

The Bedouin pride themselves as fighters, but almost every man also considers himself a poet. Literature, especially poetry recited aloud, has always been the most important Arab art. A man who can use language well and quote lines of poetry or passages from the Koran is much respected.

The poems, some of them contemporary and some handed down by past generations, are about battles, love affairs, and the hardships of the desert. The Bedouins chant them to the music of the *radaba*, a one-string violin.

Music is one art in which the old forms are still very much alive. Arab music is much more complicated than that of the West. Western music has tones and half tones, but Arab music also has quarter tones. Arab composers have about 120 different scales to choose from, and 30 to 40 of them are in common use. One of the most important Arab musical instruments is the lute, which was first brought to Europe by the Arabs. There is also the *nay*, a shepherd's flute, and a double reed pipe called the *mizwej*, which makes a sound like bagpipes. The most complicated instrument is the *ganun*, a flat board with 72 strings that sounds something like a harp.

The embroidery found on abayas and kaftans is another native art. The other main handicrafts are brasswork and heavy gold and silver jewelry. Brasswork is used for a variety of utensils, such as coffeepots and round tabletops with intricate designs marked on them. The gold and silver jewelry is a traditional wedding present, and is brought out mainly to wear at weddings. One common wedding gift of village people is jewelry made of gold coins; it is decorative and also gives the bride her own money. These small, often intricately decorated works of art are a heritage of the past, when every object that was used and treasured also had to be easily transportable by camel or horseback while the Arabs roamed their lands.

A HISTORY OF INVASIONS

Jordan is an ancient territory. Since prehistoric times, this region has existed alternately as a center of civilization and as a scarred battleground.

Traces of a highly developed civilization go back thousands of years to the early Bronze Age. At later periods, this was the area spoken of in the Bible as Transjordan, which simply means the land lying on the eastern side of the Bible's River Jordan, "trans" — or across — the Jordan. It was the home of the Old Testament peoples known as the Edomites, Moabites, Ammonites, and Amorites.

The Nabataeans, an Arab people, ruled the area from their capital city, Petra, just before the time of Christ. Later, Transjordan became one of the world's great regions under Roman rule after A.D. 106. It may have been even more heavily populated then than it is today. But the Arab people maintained their own separate way of life.

Actually, there is probably no such thing as a pure Arab. For practical purposes today, anyone who speaks Arabic and calls him- or herself an Arab is considered to be an Arab. By a stricter definition, an Arab is an Arabic-speaking nomadic desert person. In this sense, the Bedouin of Jordan and other Arabian desert and steppe regions are among the purest Arabs, even though they surely carry blood of other ancient peoples.

Certainly the most important event in the area's history, whose influence is still felt today, was the rise of the Arab Muslims in the seventh century.

MOHAMMED

Mohammed was born in 570 in Saudi Arabia. When he was about forty years old, he experienced what he believed to be a vision of God himself. God spoke to him, and Mohammed recorded what he was told in the Koran, the great holy book of the Muslim religion. The first and greatest law is that there is only one true God — Allah. Like the earlier conversion to Christianity of the Roman Empire's people, Islam (another name for the Muslim movement) was both a religious and political force, and it affected every part of its followers' lives.

ISLAM

Sweeping through the entire Middle East, Islam soon became a part of life in Transjordan. Religion is to this day a serious matter to most Muslims. Islam is a complete and coherent system in which the spiritual and worldly lives are bonded. If Muslims perform good acts, it is not just because they feel they should; it is because they are following the laws of their religion.

The laws are written in the Koran and are also handed down as part of tradition. Various Muslim sects may disagree about some of the rules, but they all believe in upholding the "Five Pillars of Faith." The five pillars are fasting during a month-long period called Ramadan; going — at least once in one's lifetime if possible — on the *hajj*, or pilgrimage to Mecca; giving alms to help the poor; praying regularly; and reciting the creed as it is given in the Koran.

Everywhere in Jordan there are mosques, the Islamic houses of worship, with their graceful soaring minarets, or towers. Five times each day, the *muezzin*, the "caller to prayer," climbs to the top of a minaret and chants his call. Muslims face toward Mecca, bow and kneel, touch their foreheads to the ground, and recite prayers to Allah. Muslims may pray anywhere, alone or with others, but it is best, Mohammed said, to pray in the mosque with other Muslims.

Although Islam is sometimes a stern religion, Muslim festivals have a light side. The two most important festivals in Jordan are the *Id Al Fitr* and the *Id Al Adha*. Either may be referred to as simply the "*Id*," or time of feasting.

Fitr means breaking the fast, and Id Al Fitr comes at the end of Ramadan. The month of Ramadan begins and ends with the sighting of the new moon. During the day in Ramadan, all Muslims are expected to abstain from food and drink. In most towns, an old cannon is fired at sunrise and again at sunset, when Mus-

lims can eat and drink until the following morning. When Ramadan finally ends, there is general rejoicing, and the Id Al Fitr lasts for three or four days.

Adha means sacrifice, and the Id Al Adha comes at the time of celebrating the hajj, when pilgrims sacrifice a live animal. Even those who are not on the pilgrimage sacrifice an animal, usually a sheep. Traditionally, one-third is given to the poor, one-third is for hospitality, to be served to friends, and one-third is for the family itself. A few days before the festival begins, you can see sheep tethered in backyards all over Jordan. The Id Al Adha also lasts three or four days.

Muslim children look forward to the two Ids in the same way Western Christian children look forward to Christmas or, in the United States, to the Fourth of July. The streets are decorated with vivid banners, and children and grownups set off fireworks. There are special early morning prayer services, and long chanting prayers can be heard from the mosques. The first day of the Id is usually devoted to the family. Presents, especially new clothes, are exchanged. On the following days there is a great deal of visiting back and forth, and everyone goes on picnics or outings.

Besides these two main festivals, there are other Muslim holy days that are also times for celebration in Jordan. The most impor-

Like many mosques, this example of contemporary Islamic architecture was built by a devout Muslim in gratitude to Allah.

tant are Mohammed's birthday and the Muslim New Year, both one-day holidays. Again, the streets are decorated and fireworks are set off.

THE SPREAD OF THE EMPIRE

By the time of the prophet's death in the year 632, Islam had become the dominant political movement in the Mid-East. A generation later, the Arab kingdom covered an area from Arabia through Syria, Iraq, and Persia, and west across North Africa, from Egypt to Tunisia. In the following century, it reached from northern India to Spain.

This great empire gradually declined, losing its political power in area after area. But the Arabs themselves have kept their identity. They think of themselves as one people, from Iraq in the East to Morocco in the West.

AFTER THE MUSLIM EMPIRE

After the middle of the eleventh century, the Arab empire slowly fell apart. The Turks came from central Asia and invaded the Arab countries. They became the leaders of the Empire. From the eleventh century to the thirteenth century, the Crusaders, Christian armies from Europe, tried to take the Holy Land but were driven back by the fierce Arab warriors.

In 1516, the Ottoman Turks conquered the whole area. But they ruled from captured cities and never had much real direct influence on the desert peoples. Their rule lasted for 400 years, and the Arabs wanted to be free.

TOWARD INDEPENDENCE

Independence finally came during World War I, in what is now called the Arab Revolt. The revolt is often remembered in the West because of the exploits of the English agent T.E. Lawrence, called Lawrence of Arabia, who led Arab guerrilla fighters on raids against the Turks. But it was, in fact, much more than that.

The British wanted help fighting against the Turks, one of their enemies in the war. With British advice and aid, Sharif Hussein Ibn Ali of the Hashemite family plotted to overthrow the Turks. His sons became military commanders. They drove the Turks out of the Hejaz, and then moved north into Transjordan and up into what are now the nations of Iraq and Syria. They were especially effective in cutting off the Turks' supply routes by destroying parts of the Hejaz Railway. At the end of the war, many people thought the Hashemites would be the leaders in what the Arabs hoped would be a united Arab nation.

But the European powers had other ideas. In secret meetings, the British and French divided much of the Middle East into their separate spheres of influence. The French would control Syria and Lebanon, and the English would have Transjordan, Palestine, and Iraq. Shortly after the war, Hussein Ibn Ali's son, Faisal, was installed by the people in Damascus as king of Syria. But the French deposed him, and the British helped to make him instead the king of Iraq. Hussein Ibn Ali himself assumed the throne in Saudi Arabia, but was soon driven into exile by his rivals, who became the rulers.

Another son of Hussein Ibn Ali, Abdullah, also wanted to rule. With a group of tough Bedouin warriors, Abdullah moved up into Transjordan, saying he was on his way to live in Syria. The English welcomed him to Transjordan, and he became the ruler under what was called the British Mandate. A man of the desert, Abdullah was equally at home with his Bedouin subjects and with Western leaders. His personal qualities, as much as anything else, enabled him to turn Jordan into a country. Abdullah brought the warring Bedouin tribes together and gave the region a sense of nationhood.

In 1946, after the Second World War, Britain ended the Mandate and recognized Transjordan as a fully independent state. Abdullah was proclaimed king. In 1948, Transjordan adopted as its official name "The Hashemite Kingdom of Jordan," after the name of the ruling family.

Then in 1951, while entering the Aqsa Mosque in the Jordanian part of Jerusalem with his sixteen-year-old grandson Hussein, King Abdullah was shot and killed by a political assassin. Hussein was not hurt because Abdullah was between him and the gunman. Hussein's father, Talal, became king. But Talal, who was said to suffer from a nervous disorder, was asked to step down so that his son could be king. In 1953, on his eighteenth birthday, Hussein became the ruler of the Hashemite Kingdom of Jordan.

THE MID-EAST CRISIS

Even before Jordan was a nation, it was part of what is today called the Mid-East crisis. This is really a continuing series of problems centering around the existence of the state of Israel and the Arabs' reaction to it.

A JEWISH HOMELAND

The Jewish people have always regarded the area of Palestine as their homeland. This is where they lived in ancient biblical times. It was the Promised Land that Moses led them to after the Exodus from Egypt. The Jewish people were among the nomad tribes that roamed the Transjordan and Palestine areas and settled in the villages. Then in A.D. 70, the Romans, as part of their rule over the region, destroyed the great Jewish temple at Jerusalem. The Jews left, in what is called the diaspora, or scattering, and settled in Europe, northern Africa, and Asia. They did not forget their homeland, though. Jewish literature includes many beautiful memories of Jerusalem. Over the centuries, Jews throughout the world continued to dream and hope that "next year, in Jerusalem," they would live on Jewish land again.

But very little was done about this until the end of the nineteenth century. Then a movement known as Zionism, led by Dr. Theodor Herzl, began to spread among Jews. This encouraged the return of Jews to Palestine to form their own country. The World Zionist Organization, founded in 1897, organized these efforts and raised funds to help the Jewish settlers. The Zionists began many Jewish communities in Palestine, founded settlements, and revived the ancient Hebrew language. This language unites Jews all over the world, as Arabic does the Arab peoples.

During World War I, when the British wanted help fighting the Turks, they appealed to the Zionists in Palestine as well as to the Arabs. In return for their help, the British government issued a document called The Balfour Declaration. In it, the British said they would support a Jewish homeland in Palestine.

After the war ended, during the years of the British Mandate, more and more Jews emigrated to Palestine. The Arabs who lived there were often uneasy about this. The Jewish emigrants were often more skilled and better educated than they were and competed with them for work. The settlers began making farms in the countryside, taking over the wild desert the Arabs loved. And, as more Jews arrived, there was more open talk of a homeland. But this could only be on land taken from the Arabs. Both groups, the Jews and the Arabs, felt they were entitled to the land. The situation became more and more tense.

Bethlehem, the birthplace of Christ, is located on the West Bank of Jordan: an area long disputed by Israelis and Arabs.

Before and during World War II, Nazi Germany began a campaign to exterminate all the Jews of Europe. Before the war ended, they had killed 6 million Jews — perhaps the worst crime of genocide, the murder of a people, ever recorded. The Jews, fleeing Europe, were more desperate than ever for a country of their own to be safe in.

Because Britain refused to let any more Jews enter Palestine, the Jews began to smuggle in people. They had to fight the British army trying to prevent it, and they began to feel they would have to fight the Arabs as well.

THE 1947 WAR

In 1947 Britain announced it would end the British Mandate the next year. In November of 1947 the United Nations voted to partition the country into separate Arab and Jewish states. The Jews would be given the areas where they were heavily settled. As soon as this decision was announced, Arabs began to attack Jewish settlements, hoping to drive the Jews off the land before the partition was made. Late in 1947, a Jewish force defeated the main Arab fighting force, and Arabs began to flee their lands. The Arabs headed for the areas nearest the Jordan River, and many crossed the Jordan as well.

On May 14, 1948, the nation of Israel came into existence. Arab armies attacked Israel, hoping to win back territory. Armies came from all the Arab countries including the Arab Legion from Jordan, probably the best Arab fighting force. They occupied the territory near the Jordan River, which became known as the West Bank. The Israelis drove back the other Arab forces, although Egypt kept control of a small strip of land in the south, on the

Mediterranean coastline, called the Gaza Strip. The war ended early in 1949, and the area was peaceful for a while.

THE 1956 WAR

The Arab countries still refused to recognize the existence of Israel. There were continual small armed fights along the borders of Israel, and many Palestinians formed commando groups that raided Jewish settlements.

In 1956 the situation worsened. The Israelis invaded the Gaza Strip area, saying they had to stop the raids made from there. The Israeli forces continued south into the Sinai desert, and it looked as if they would invade Egypt. France and Great Britain landed their own troops near the Suez Canal. The situation seemed to threaten the peace of the whole world.

Then the United Nations, with the help of the United States and Russia, stepped in. A U.N. emergency force moved into the area between the Israeli and the Arab forces, acting as a peace-keeping team. The fighting ended, and once more there was an uneasy peace.

THE 1967 WAR

In May, 1967, the U.N. withdrew its forces at the request of Egypt. On June 5, war broke out again between Israel and its Arab neighbors. The heaviest fighting was along its borders with Egypt and Jordan. But the Israelis won a quick victory. The war lasted only six days, and it is often called the Six-Day War.

Israel occupied all the West Bank territory that had belonged to Jordan. More Arab refugees fled, either to the refugee camps run by the United Nations Relief and Works Agency (UNRWA) or to Jordan itself.

These Palestinian refugees soon made up more than half the population of Jordan. They organized many Palestinian groups working for the recovery of their land. Many of the groups were peaceful, but many others were commando groups using terrorist tactics. They felt that King Hussein wasn't doing enough to help them, and they began to talk of deposing him and taking over the government themselves. Finally, in September of 1970, Hussein declared that the Palestinian groups had to leave the country. A civil war broke out, with some Jordanians supporting the Palestinian groups. But the great majority of the people were with Hussein, including most of the army with its faithful Bedouins. The king prevailed. The Palestinian groups who had fought left; many of them went north to Lebanon or Syria. Hussein imprisoned many who stayed. Most of the Palestinian refugees hadn't taken part in the fighting and remained in Jordan, living peacefully.

THE 1973 WAR

In October, 1973, another war broke out. The Arabs attacked unexpectedly on the morning of Yom Kippur, an important Jewish holiday. This is sometimes called the Yom Kippur War, or the Ramadan War, since it was also during the month of Ramadan. Again, the rest of the world became concerned, worried that the fighting would spread. And again, peace talks were convened. These were held in Geneva, Switzerland, with the United States and Russia as cochairmen.

In November, 1973, the Arabs at the peace talks agreed that the P.L.O., the largest and most powerful Palestinian group, should have the responsibility for the West Bank and its future. King Hussein agreed to this. Shortly afterward, King Hussein granted amnesty to all political prisoners in Jordan, freeing the Palestinians he had imprisoned in 1970.

THE 1977 PEACE INITIATIVE

Since the 1973 war, the uneasy peace has continued. None of the Arab countries have attacked Israel, but neither have they recognized its existence. The Mid-East Crisis seemed unending.

In late 1977 Anwar Sadat, the president of Egypt, began making a personal effort to bring peace to the area. He offered to come to Jerusalem to discuss his plans with the Israel government and people. This was a startling offer, as it was the first time an Arab leader even suggested that he would recognize Israel. The Israeli government, led by Prime Minister Menachem Begin, accepted Sadat's offer. President Sadat flew to Jerusalem and, a few weeks later, Prime Minister Begin flew to Egypt, to participate in talks there. It seemed as if peace was very near.

But then the talks bogged down, and no one was able to predict what might happen next. All sides want peace, but no one seems sure of how to make it come about.

King Hussein stayed out of the peace initiative talks. He has said that he still hopes that Israel will return the land it took in the 1967 war. But Hussein is certainly also hoping for peace to come soon so that he can turn his full attention to ruling his own country and to meeting its needs for the future.

THE COUNTRY NOW

THE KING

Hussein's Hashemite family name comes from Hashem, an ancestor of the prophet Mohammed. King Hussein is literally a direct descendant of Mohammed through the prophet's daughter Fatimah. From the seventh century until well into the twentieth, the Hashemites exercised authority in the Hejaz, the site of Islam's most holy places.

King Hussein's reign has often been precarious. Time after time there have been plots against his life. Luckily, none has succeeded. For a period, Jordan and Iraq, under the young King Faisal, grandson of Abdullah's brother, moved toward unity. They merged their diplomatic corps and military commands. But in 1958 Faisal, who was about the same age as Hussein, was killed in a revolution that ended Hashemite rule in Iraq. Since then, Jordan has been the only Hashemite nation.

Hussein has proved to be very good at juggling his country's various political forces. He has usually spared his enemies after he has outwitted them. But he has also proved himself capable of ruthless action, as he showed after the 1970 civil war.

Hussein is extremely popular with many of his people; he is admired for his political and military skills as well as for his dashing personal style. Like a desert Bedouin sheik, he personally commands his armed forces. He is an avid sportsman who enjoys water skiing and pilots jet aircraft. Sometimes passengers on Alia, the Royal Jordanian Airline (named for his eldest daughter), discover that their king is at the controls.

Hussein has two sons and three daughters. He has been married four times, first to a Hashemite cousin, then to the daughter of a British military advisor, and then to a Palestinian woman, who was also named Alia. Some people felt that the marriage of a Hashemite king to a west Jordanian helped to reconcile the country's factions. Queen Alia was killed on February 2, 1977, in a helicopter crash, however, and in June, 1978 he married Elizabeth Halaby, an American.

THE GOVERNMENT

Legally, Jordan is a constitutional monarchy. The king approves laws and promulgates them — puts them into effect simply by announcing them. He has the power to declare war, to make peace, and to sign treaties.

He also has the right to convene and adjourn the Jordanian Parliament. The parliament has two houses, the Senate and the

Chamber of Deputies. They were dissolved by the king in 1974. On February 5, 1977, he reconvened them. Many Palestinians protested, however, because they said the fact that the parliament contained members representing the West Bank went against the agreement that the P.L.O. represented that area. So Hussein dissolved Parliament again on February 7. He also dissolved the Arab National Union, which had been the country's only political organization since 1971.

SOCIAL SERVICES

The main cities and population centers in Jordan all have government hospitals at which any Jordanian can be treated for very little money. There are also government health clinics in every town of any size. Altogether, there are probably at least a thousand physicians working in Jordan.

Some of the nurses are foreigners since conservative families in Arab countries have not considered nursing a suitable profession for women. But such prejudices are disappearing, and Jordanian nurses are now found all over the country. There has never been any prejudice against women doctors, partly because tradition-bound Arab men prefer that their wives and daughters be seen by women doctors.

Women can be found in nearly all goverment offices and in many private companies. Increasing numbers of young women have become teachers. And one area where women are employed

His Majesty King Hussein

frequently is in radio and television broadcasting. Many directors and announcers are women.

Jordan has its own Institute of Social Work, which trains about thirty men and women each year. There are a number of projects to aid the handicapped. In the countryside, youth clubs that provide training in agriculture are being established. And there are now some two hundred nutrition clinics throughout the country.

EDUCATION

Some of the schools in Jordan are privately operated, usually by religious groups. In the refugee camps UNRWA operates elementary schools for the children of displaced Palestinians. But 70 percent of Jordan's students are attending free government schools. Girls as well as boys are now going to school, which is a major break with the old Arab views about women staying at home.

All Jordanians must attend school from the ages of seven to sixteen. Classes are conducted in Arabic, but English is taught to everyone beginning in the fifth grade. Most elementary and secondary school pupils attend separate schools for girls and boys, with men teaching the boys and women teaching the girls. The three-year junior high schools prepare students for higher education and give courses in home economics for girls and vocational training for boys. The general high schools prepare academic students for college, and special vocational high schools have commercial, industrial, and agricultural programs.

Most students who go on to college or university go abroad. Most of them go to colleges in the surrounding Arab nations, but some go to Europe or the United States. The University of Jordan,

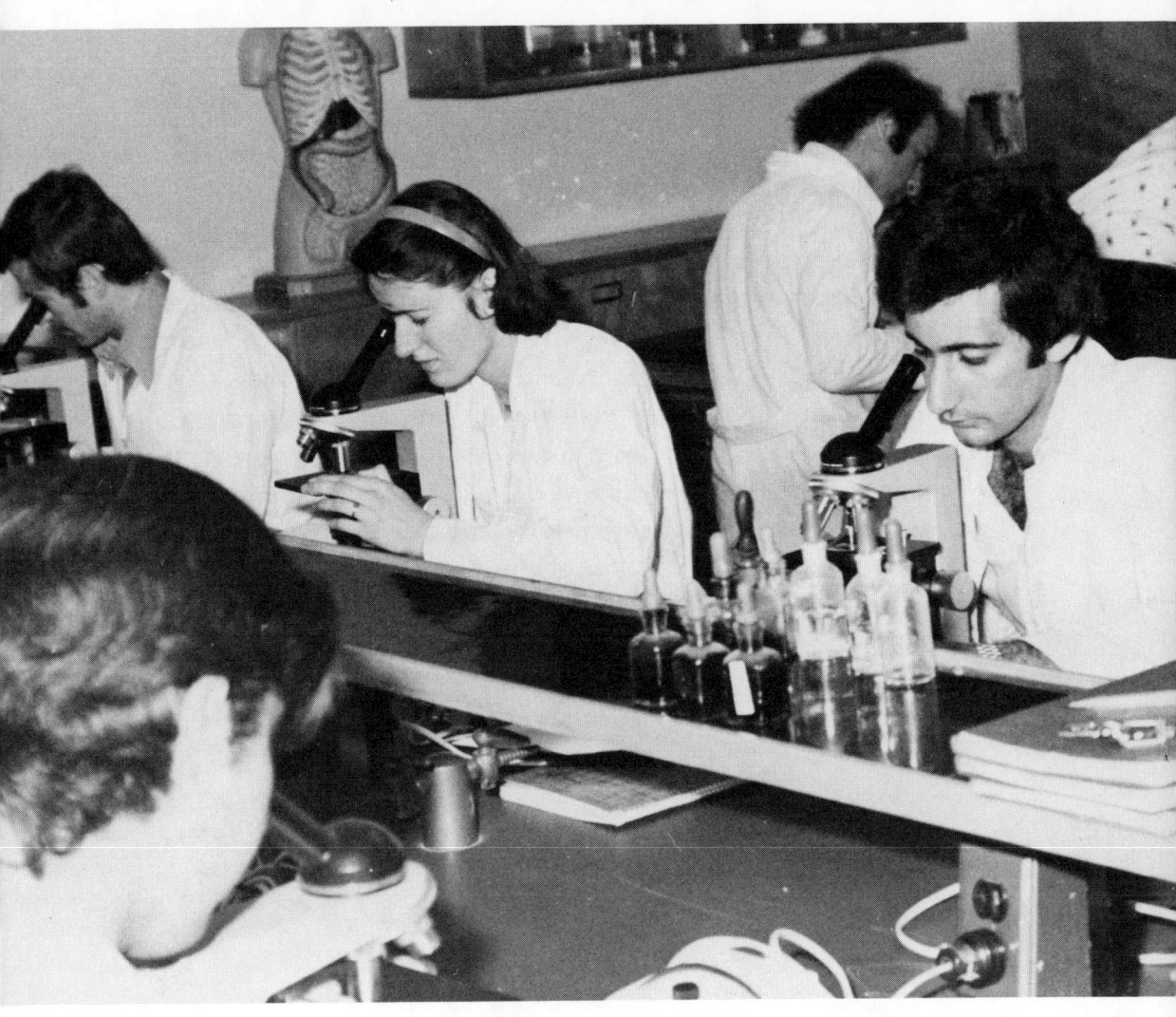

A biology class at the University of Jordan. More and more women are receiving formal education and, as a result, are finding work outside the home when they graduate.

in Amman, was founded in 1962. It now offers liberal arts courses with degrees in science, economics, and commerce as well as in medicine and law.

COMMUNICATIONS

Jordan is very much a modern nation in its understanding of the importance of communications. There are only a few newspapers in Jordan, but most people see at least one of them. The government operates two radio stations and two television channels. One of the stations and one of the channels are devoted to foreign language broadcasts, mostly in English, but with some French and German programs. The skyline of Amman bristles with TV antennas, and transistor radios and cassette tape players are now found everywhere, even carried by Bedouins deep in the desert.

One of the country's most interesting new landmarks is a great half-shell pointed at the sky, north of Amman. It is Jordan's tracking station, which links the country's telephone system to communications space satellites, for rapid communications with all parts of the world.

THE FUTURE

In today's Jordan there are many signs of a young and vigorous state. The cities are growing at a rapid rate. Schools and other public buildings are being built everywhere. Small industries are expanding. Many major public works projects for irrigating the land are being developed.

Although on the surface Jordan has become quite Western, important elements of the past remain very much alive. The family structure is still strong. Juvenile delinquency is almost unheard of in Jordan. The sheiks still carry enormous influence in the nation's affairs. All real political power is held by King Hussein, who is backed by loyal sheiks, the powerful army, and Bedouin fighting men. Jordan is officially an Islamic state at a time when few nations are officially connected with a religion.

The University of Jordan was established at Amman in
1962 with a total of 167 students. Enrollment today
is over 6000, and one third of the students are women.

But it is still far from certain that Jordan will be able to realize the goals it has set for itself. Much work remains to be done. For example, it is still hard just to ensure that everyone has enough to eat. Jordan still must import much of its food. The Red Sea contains many fish, but there is no modern fishing fleet operating out of Aqaba to catch them. Scientists have located several underground water resources beneath the desert, which could be used to irrigate new cropland, but it will be difficult and expensive to develop them.

In the political area, even greater tasks lie before Jordan. Few people think that, even with the latest peace efforts, it will be easy to solve the Mid-East crisis. There is still the Palestinian problem, with refugees torn between trying to return to their former homes or deciding to build a new life where they are. And the Bedouin way of life, which most of the people were following only one generation ago, has nearly disappeared. Cars and trucks have replaced the camel, and life will never be the same for the people of the desert.

Jordan's future will not be easy. The land itself is still harsh. Cultivated land is spreading, but the desert still remains. The Jordanian people look to a future of change. But, just as much, they take their inspiration from the past. The Arab culture, the Bedouin independence, the Palestinian way of life — all are blending together to make a new Jordan. The problems change, but the people and the land remain.

FOR FURTHER READING

Caldwell, John C. *Let's Visit the Middle East*. New York: John Day, 1972.

Copeland, Paul W. *The Land and People of Jordan*. Philadelphia: J. B. Lippincott, 1965.

Edmonds, I. G. *Islam*. New York: Franklin Watts, 1977.

Henderson, Larry. *The Arab Middle East*. New York: Thomas Nelson, 1970.

Miller, David W., and Moore, Clark D., eds. *The Middle East Yesterday and Today*. New York: Praeger Publishers, 1970.

Stegmuller, Camille Mirepoix. *Jordan in Pictures*. New York: Sterling Publishing Co., 1974.

INDEX

(59)